CREATIVE VEN

The Future

Written by Rebecca Stark

Educational Impressions

ISBN: 0-910857-48-2

© Educational Impressions, Inc. 1987

EDUCATIONAL IMPRESSIONS, INC.
Hawthorne, NJ 07507

Cover Design and Illustrations by Karen Neulinger

Table of Contents

TO THE TEACHER 4
WILLIAMS' MODEL 5

What's the Problem 6
Priorities 7
Going Places 8
Future Digs 9
Table Talk 10
The Best of Me 11
Who's Who of the 21st Century 12
Decisions, Decisions 13
A Change for the Better 14
I'll Smile Tomorrow 15
The Computers Are Coming! 16
Trends 17
Future Headlines 18
Class Reunion 19
Future Fads 20
Generation Gap 21
Functional Fixity 22
Proud Grandparent 23
Mr./Ms. President 24
Clones 25
An Interview 26
This Is the Life! 27
The Joys of Parenthood 28
Roles to Play 29
A Spy in the Family 30
A New National Passtime 31
What's Going on? 32
Now What Do We Do with Them? 33

Why Should I Study That? 34
As Principal 35
1 + 1 = 1 36
If You Could 37
Sticky Situations 38
A Perfect Roommate 39
What's the Question? 40
My Home Town 41
How Would It Feel? 42
Super Similes 43
F-U-T-U-R-E Artists 44
Where Did the Time Go? 45
A Better School Desk 46
Madame President 47
A Different Breed 48
Our Changing Vocabulary 49
Shuttle Service 50
Time Capsule 51
Hypothesize 52
Ask a Seer 53
Modern Flicks 54
Planning Helps 55
Analogies 56
New Frontiers 57
Evolution 58
Resolutions 59
I Need a Change 60
An Acrostic 61
What If? 62

FOLLOW-UP ACTIVITIES 63-64

To The Teacher

The open-ended activities in this book were designed to extend the imagination and creativity of your students and to encourage students to examine their feelings and values. Specifically, they focus upon the cognitive and affective pupil behaviors described in Williams' Model: fluent thinking, flexible thinking, original thinking, elaborative thinking, risk-taking, complexity, curiosity and imagination. (See the summary of Williams' Model on page 5.)

Students must learn to recognize problems and to produce and consider a variety of alternate solutions to those problems. Teachers, therefore, should urge students to defer judgment of their ideas until they have produced many alternatives. They should also encourage them to let their imaginations run wild so that their ideas include clever, unusual alternatives as well as the more obvious ones.

Each volume of the **CREATIVE VENTURES SERIES** centers around a different area; however, the area is broad and the nature of the activities is interdisciplinary.

I hope you and your students enjoy your ventures into creativity!

Rebecca Stark

A SUMMARY OF WILLIAMS' MODEL

COGNITIVE-INTELLECTIVE

Fluent thinking— to generate a great number of relevant responses.

Flexible thinking— to take different approaches in order to generate different categories of thought.

Original thinking— to think in novel or unique ways in order to produce unusual responses and clever ideas.

Elaborative thinking— to add on to, or embellish upon, an idea.

AFFECTIVE-FEELING

Risk-taking— to have courage to expose yourself to failure or criticism and to defend your ideas.

Complexity— to be challenged to seek alternatives and to delve into intricate problems or ideas.

Curiosity— to be inquisitive and to be willing to follow hunches just to see what will happen.

Imagination— to feel intuitively and to reach beyond sensual or real boundaries.

What's the Problem?

Sometimes we must look at a problem differently in order to recognize the real problem.

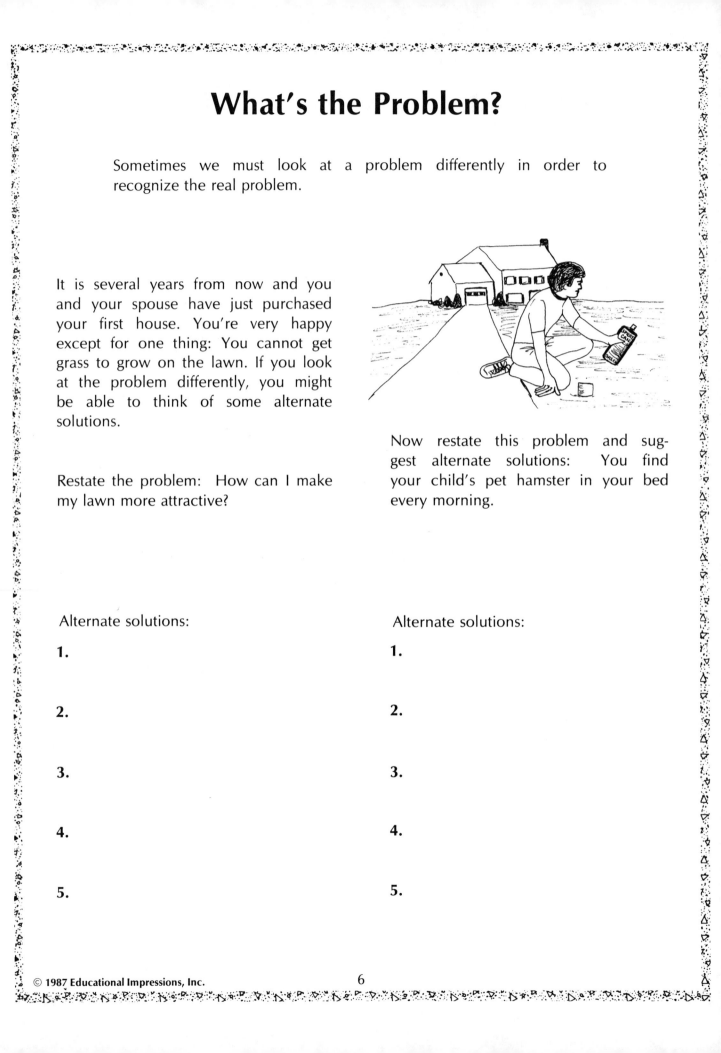

It is several years from now and you and your spouse have just purchased your first house. You're very happy except for one thing: You cannot get grass to grow on the lawn. If you look at the problem differently, you might be able to think of some alternate solutions.

Restate the problem: How can I make my lawn more attractive?

Now restate this problem and suggest alternate solutions: You find your child's pet hamster in your bed every morning.

Alternate solutions:

1.

2.

3.

4.

5.

Alternate solutions:

1.

2.

3.

4.

5.

Priorities

Setting priorities is a necessary aspect of planning for the future.

Make a list of all the things you hope to accomplish this week.

Now list them in the order of importance to you.

Going Places

Invent a new form of transportation.

How will it run?

How many passengers will fit?

In what ways is it new?

In what ways is it better than other forms of transportation?

Draw a
picture
of it!

Future Digs

It is the year 4000. Some future archaeologists have just unearthed the following artifacts. Looking at these artifacts from their perspective, hypothesize as to the functions of each item.

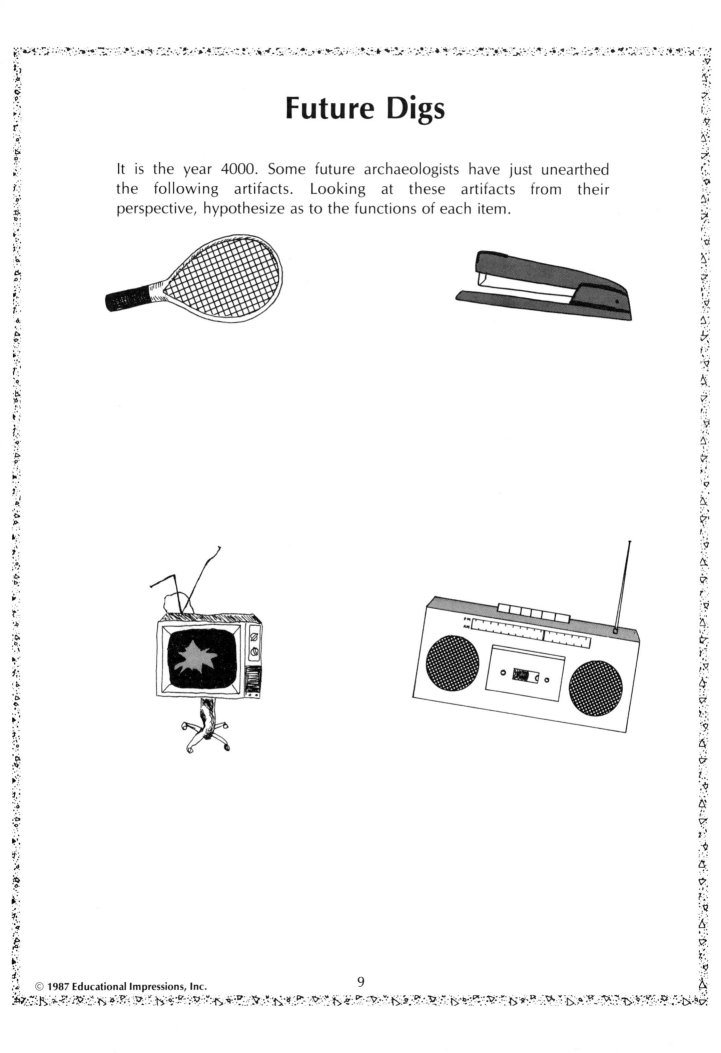

Table Talk

You have been caught in a time warp and find yourself at the dinner table with a family of the 25th Century. Think of questions to ask each member of the family.

List as many questions for each member of the family as you can.

The Best of Me

Suppose it becomes possible to choose which of your traits (personality traits as well as physical ones) and which of your spouse's traits are to be passed on to your offspring.

I think I'd like the child to have my eyes.

Which of your traits would you want your child to inherit?

What traits would you like your spouse to have?

Which of your traits would you *not* want your son or daughter to inherit?

Do you want all of the traits you hope to find in your future spouse to be passed on to your offspring? Tell why or why not.

Who's Who
of the
Twenty-first Century

Plan a "Who's Who of the Twenty-first Century" booklet. In it you will describe the future accomplishments of your friends, classmates and relatives.

	People	Major Accomplishments
1.		
2.		
3.		
4.		
5.		
6.		
7.		
8.		
9.		
10.		

Decisions, Decisions!

Make a list of all the decisions you made last week that have had an effect upon what happened (or will happen) this week.

Hmm... Should I study or watch TV?

	Decision	Effect
1.		
2.		
3.		
4.		
5.		
6.		
7.		
8.		
9.		
10.		

A Change for the Better

List all the ways in which you would like to see the world change in the future. Consider political, medical, scientific, educational and social aspects.

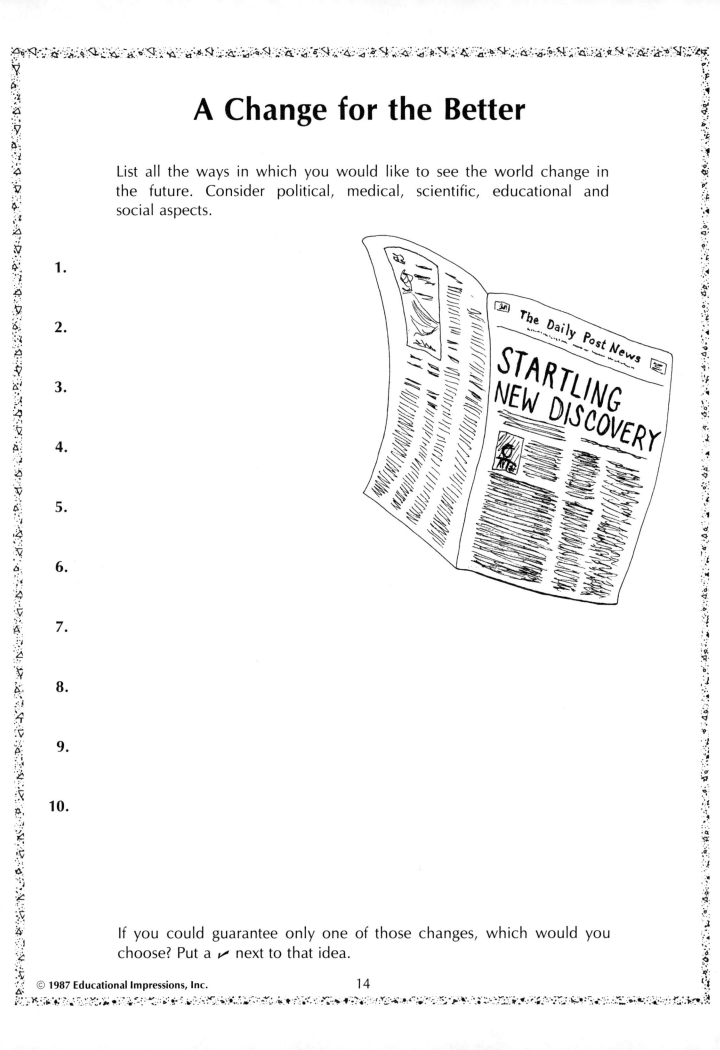

1.

2.

3.

4.

5.

6.

7.

8.

9.

10.

If you could guarantee only one of those changes, which would you choose? Put a ✔ next to that idea.

I'll Smile Tomorrow

What are all the things you could do today that would make you happy tomorrow?

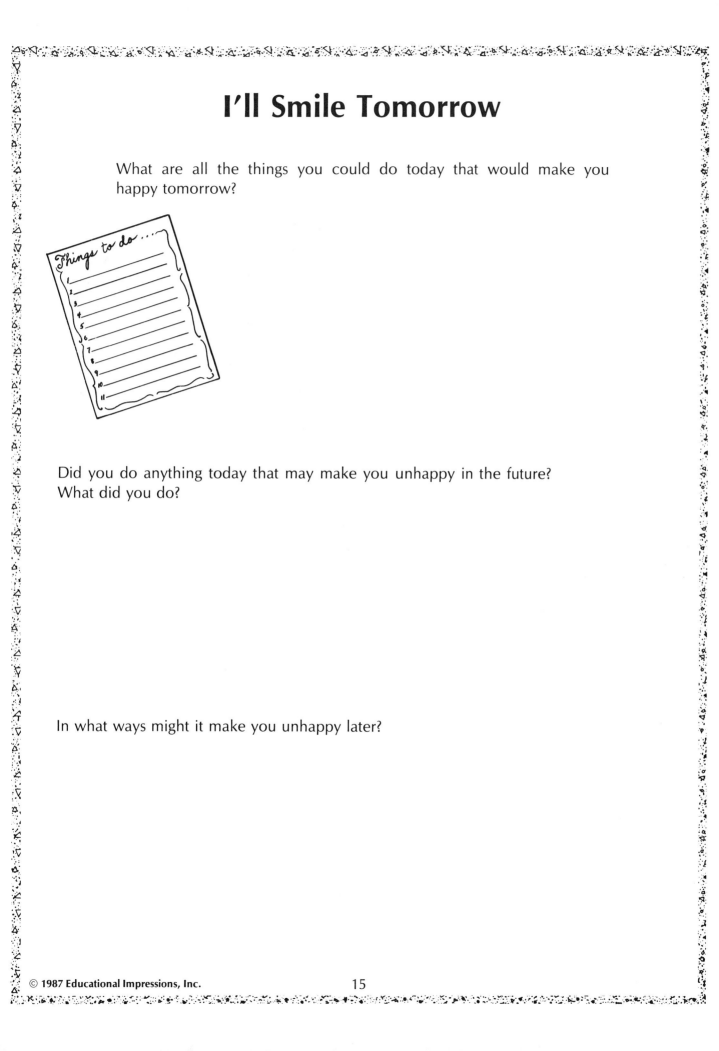

Did you do anything today that may make you unhappy in the future?
What did you do?

In what ways might it make you unhappy later?

Here Come the Computers

Some people fear that in the future too much of our lives will be controlled by computers.

TAKE TWO ASPIRINS
AND CALL ME
IN THE MORNING

What if doctors were replaced by computers?

What if a robot were elected President?

What if your teacher were a computer?

Trends

In order to plan for the future, we often study trends. More people own video cassette recorders (VCR's) than they did a year ago. That is a trend. Can you think of any other trends? Name as many as you can!

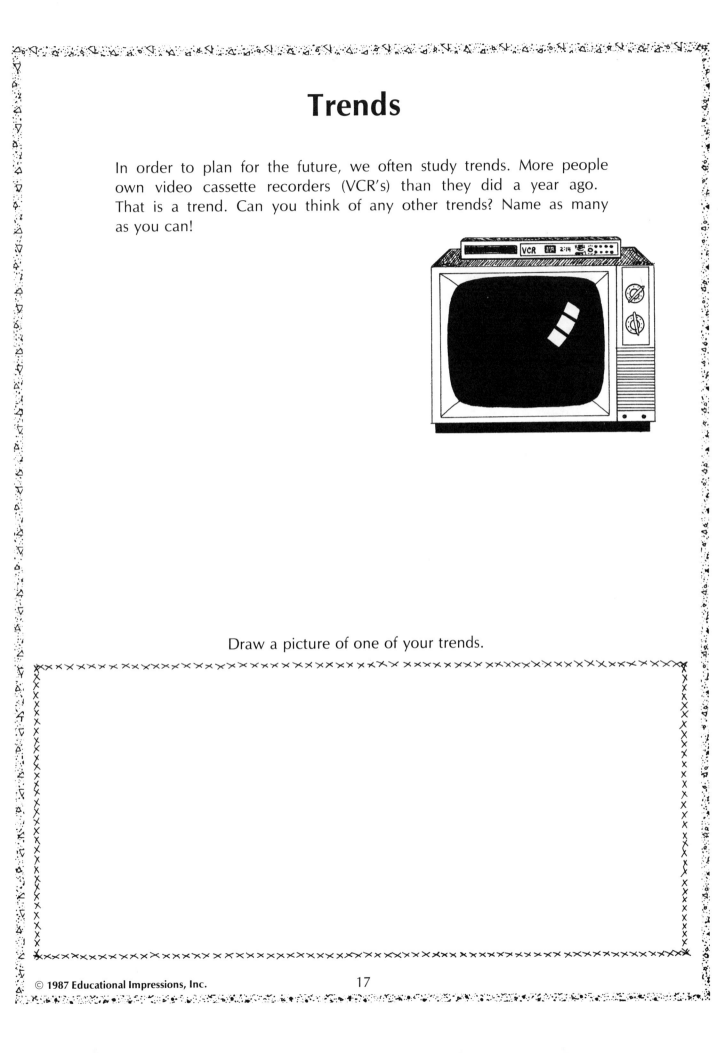

Draw a picture of one of your trends.

Future Headlines

Imagine that the following are headlines of the future. For each, summarize at least three possible events behind the headlines.

Visitors Receive Warm Welcome

New Form of Energy Discovered

Amendment Added to Constitution

Class Reunion

You are at your tenth high school reunion. You and your friends are reminiscing about the "good old days."

List all the occurrences that took place in your elementary and high school years about which you will reminisce. (Some of these events might not yet have occurred!)

Future Fads

Fads are things or fashions that are very popular and taken up with great enthusiasm for a brief period of time.   Hula hoops and pet rocks are two fads of the past.

Out of these circles, invent fads of the future. Name each and give a brief expanation of what it is.

Generation Gap

For each situation define the problem and list as many alternate solutions as you can.

Your 18-year-old daughter wants to quit college to join the circus.

Problem:

Alternatives:

You learn that your 16-year-old son has been shoplifting.

Problem:

Alternatives:

Your friends and business associates can never reach you on the phone. It's always busy. You've asked your son and daughter to limit their calls, but to no avail.

Problem:

Alternatives:

You surprise the family by announcing a vacation to Niagara Falls. You've been looking forward to a family vacation, but your children do not seem anxious to join you.

Problem:

Alternatives:

Functional Fixity

When we think of objects in a set way (as having a particular use), it is called functional fixity, or functional fixedness. Sometimes, in order to solve problems, we must think of new ways to use familiar objects. For example, this boy has attached his chewing gum to a piece of string in order to retrieve a coin that has fallen through the grating.

For each of these familiar objects, think of some out-of-the-ordinary uses.

Yardstick:

Table:

Sweater:

Books:

Coffee pot:

Drinking glass:

Chair:

Newspaper:

Proud Grandparent

Imagine that it is sometime in the future and that you have just become a grandparent for the first time. List as many adjectives as you can that describe how you feel.

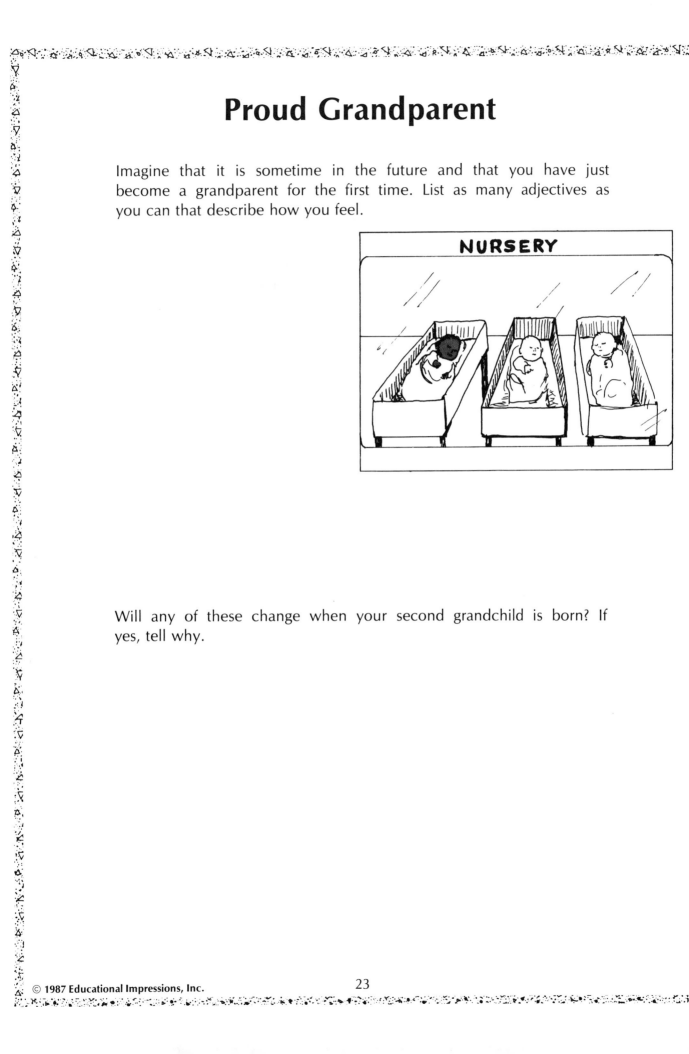

Will any of these change when your second grandchild is born? If yes, tell why.

Mr./Ms. President

You have just been elected President. What would you like to see accomplished during your term of office?

Clones

It is the future and scientists are able to clone human beings. (To clone is to create a genetic duplicate of an individual organism through asexual reproduction, such as by stimulating a single cell.)

Record as many reasons as you can think of to clone humans (ethical or not).

List as many adjectives as you can think of that would describe how you would feel if you learned that you were a clone.

Write two letters to the editor of a newspaper which comment upon the ethics of cloning from two different points of view.

Dear Editor:

Dear Editor:

Sincerely,

Sincerely,

An Interview

You have become an admissions officer at a major university. Think of as many questions as you can to ask prospective students during an interview.

This Is the Life!

Make a list of all the things you would like to do after you retire.

The Joys of Parenthood

Imagine yourself the parent of a 5-year-old. How would you feel and what would you do in each of the following situations.

First day of school:

Child comes home crying because classmate has called him/her dumb.

Child has lead in Mother's Day play:

Child tells you he/she hates you because he/she can't go to the park alone:

Roles to Play

From the time we are born until the time we die, we play a great number of roles. A role is the customary behavior associated with a particular status. For example, you play one role as a student, another as a son or daughter, and still another if you are a brother or sister.

What roles do you now play?

What roles will you play:

15 years from now?   **25 years from now?**   **40 years from now?**

A Spy in the Family

You expected some problems in your marriage, but you weren't prepared for this! You just learned that your spouse has been spying against your government in behalf of a foreign nation. State your problem and list your alternatives.

Problem:

Alternatives:

Which alternative do you think you would choose?

Would you choose a different alternative if it were your child instead of your spouse? Why or why not?

A New National Passtime

Create a totally new sport or combine two now popular sports to create a new one.

What is the main objective?

How many on a team?

How many teams play at once?

How is it scored?

What are the special rules?

What equipment is needed?

Describe the uniforms.

Are any safety precautions necessary?

In what ways, if any, is it like other sports?

What's Going On?

Assume that it is several years from now and that you have just been handed the morning newspaper. On the front page is the following picture with directions to turn to page 8 for the story. You turn the pages, but page 8 is missing. You call the newspaper office to find out what's happening. What questions will you ask in order to gain information not obtainable merely by looking at the picture?

You are about to do the grocery shopping for your family. As you enter the supermarket, you find the following scene. What questions will you ask the shop owner to find out what's happening?

Now What Do We Do with Them?

Suppose these everyday objects were to become obsolete in terms of their current functions? Think of new ways to use the items so that you don't have to throw them away.

Pens & Pencils

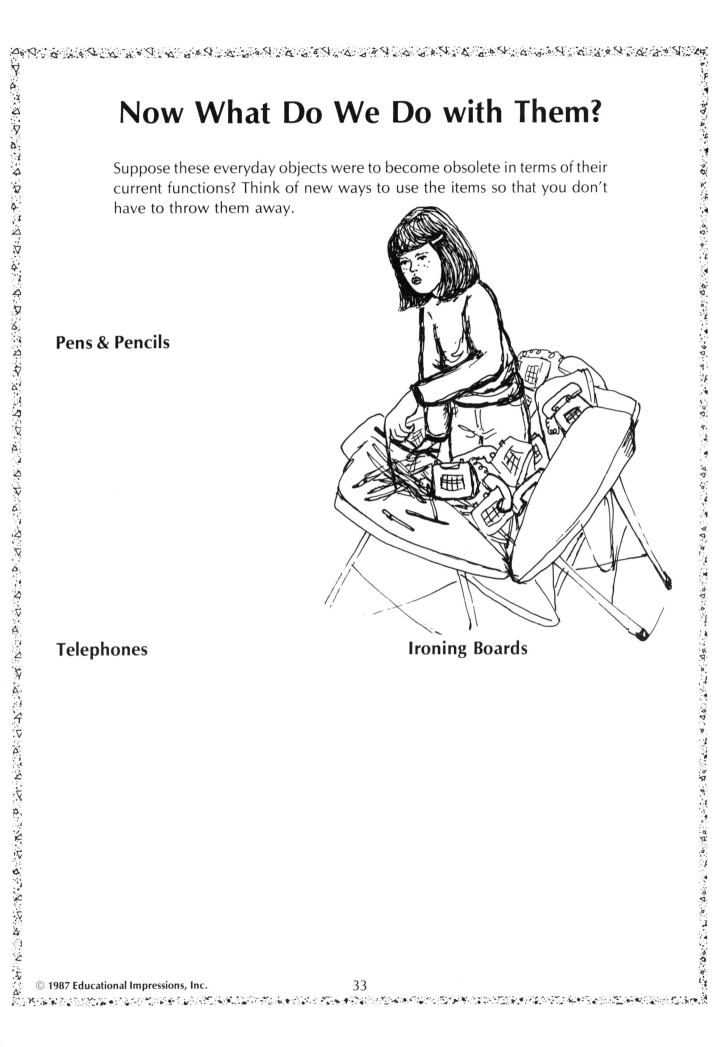

Telephones

Ironing Boards

Why Should I Study That?

Tell how each of the subjects you are currently studying in school may help you in later years.

Subject   **Will Help Me...**

As Principal...

What if you were to become principal of your school? What changes would you recommend to make your school a better place in which to teach and learn?

I would recommend these changes to make our school a better place in which to teach:

I would recommend these changes to make our school a better place in which to learn:

1 + 1 = 1

Combine two objects to make another, more useful object. For example, a clock and a radio were combined to make the now common clock-radio!

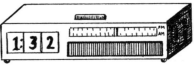

List the attributes (qualities) of object #1:

List the attributes (qualities) of object #2:

For each put a ✔ next to those attributes you want to keep.

List the attributes of your new object:

Draw a picture of your new object:

If You Could...

If you could choose any career in the world, which would you choose? Why?

If you could visit any place in the world, where would you go? Why?

If you could look like anyone in the world, whom would you like to look like? Why?

If you could be as smart as anyone in the world, whom would you choose? Why?

If you could live anywhere in the world, where would you live? Why?

If you could have dinner with anyone in the world, with whom would you dine? Why?

If you could invent anything in the world, what would you invent? Why?

Sticky Situations

Situation #1:

Your boss invites you home for dinner. The main course is shrimp scampi. You are highly allergic to shrimp. State your problem and list your alternatives.

Situation #2:

Your best friend decides to run for office and asks you to be campaign manager. You don't think that he/she is qualified for the job. State your problem and list your alternatives.

Situation #3:

You know that your friend has been shoplifting. He/she asks you to go with him/her to the shopping mall. State your problem and list your alternatives.

A Perfect Roommate

You are about to enter college as a freshman. You receive a form that asks you to list the qualities you would like your roommate to have.

List the adjectives and phrases that describe your idea of a perfect roommate.

Review the list you just compiled. Number the items in the list in their order of importance to you. Now put a ✔ next to those qualities which *you do not* possess.

What's the Question?

It is the year 2025 and you are being interviewed. The following statements are your replies to the interviewer's questions. For each, think of as many situations as you can to which the reply might refer.

"It was difficult, but it was worth the trouble."

"I was really surprised when they announced my name."

"I'm not sure I would do it again."

"I did it in self-defense!"

"Well, it's one of my few regrets."

My Home Town

You are 70 years old. You haven't seen your home town in over 50 years — until now! You've brought your young grandchild to see the town where you were raised, but everything's changed.

Describe the changes that have taken place as if spoken to your grandchild.

"_____

_____

_____

_____

_____

_____

_____

_____

_____

_____

_____

_____

_____

_____ "

Still from the perspective of yourself at 70, circle those changes which you feel are an improvement over the way things were.

How Would It Feel?

Describe how it would feel to be...

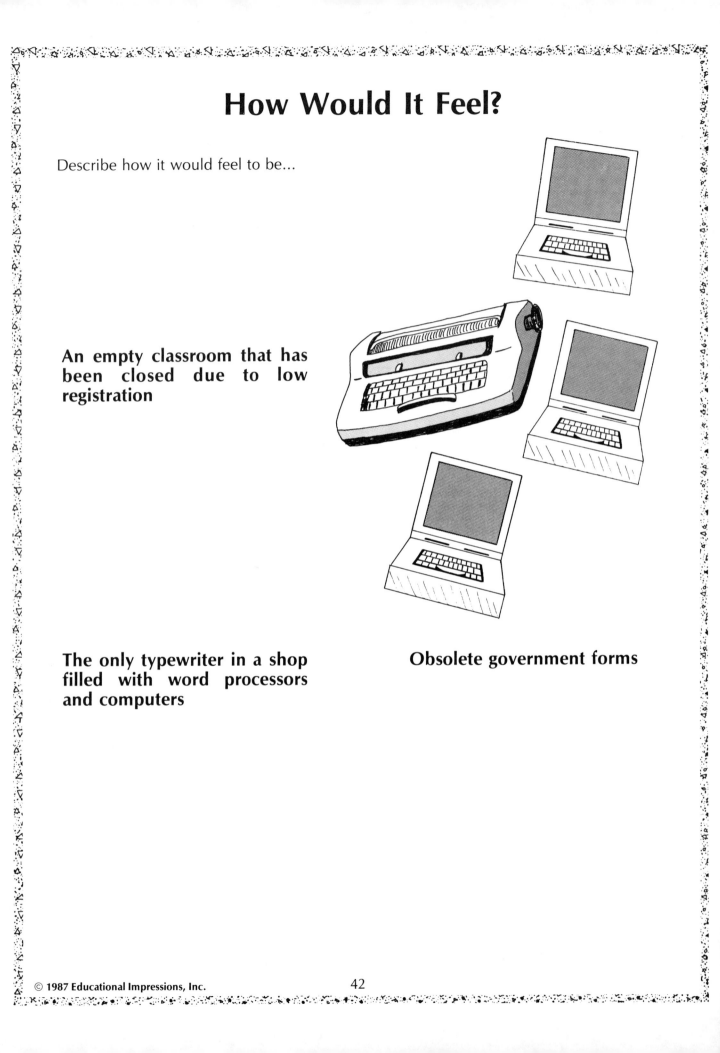

An empty classroom that has been closed due to low registration

The only typewriter in a shop filled with word processors and computers

Obsolete government forms

Super Similes

Complete each simile from the point of view of someone living in the year 2200. Try to think of some unique ideas!

As modern as _____

As ancient as _____

As valuable as _____

As dangerous as _____

As _____ as a frisbee

As _____ as a pet rock

As _____ as _____

As _____ as _____

As _____ as _____

43

F-U-T-U-R-E Artists

See how many pictures you can make from the letters F-U-T-U-R-E. Try to make them interesting and have them tell as complete a story as possible. Name each.

F   U

T   U

R   E

Where Did the Time Go?

It's your twenty-fifth wedding anniversary. You look at your photograph album and begin to reminisce about the past 25 years. You think about your family...your friends...your education...your career. You think about what you have done, how you have felt, events you have witnessed and your dreams — both fulfilled and unfulfilled.

Write down your thoughts and feelings in the form of a soliloquy. A soliloquy is a literary or dramatic form of discourse in which a character talks to him/herself or reveals his/her thoughts in the form of a monologue without a listener.

"_____

_____

_____

_____

_____

_____

_____

_____

_____

_____"

A Better School Desk

How can you make a school desk better for future generations? What can you add? Eliminate? Make larger? Make smaller? Rearrange? Borrow from something else?

Draw a picture of your
new, improved desk.

Madame President

As of the writing of this activity, there has never been a female president of the United States of America. (A female, Geraldine Ferraro, did run for the office of vice-president in the 1984 election.)

Think about how it would feel to be the first female president of the United States. Then, pretending to be her, write an entry in your diary for the evening following your election.

Dear Diary,

Now think about how it would feel to be her husband. Write an entry in a diary from his point of view.

Dear Diary,

A Different Breed

Create a new animal derived by cloning 2 different animals. (To clone is to create a genetic duplicate of an individual organism through asexual reproduction — for example, by stimulating a single cell.)

List the attributes, or
qualities, of animal #1

List the attributes, or
qualities, of animal #2

List the attributes, or
qualities, of your new animal.

Name your new animal and draw its picture.

_____

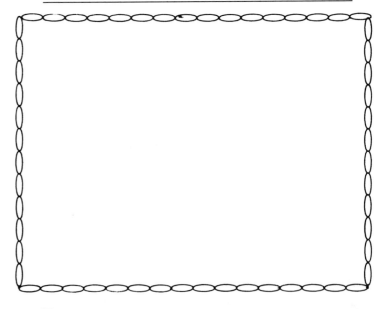

Our Changing Vocabulary

From time to time new words become part of our vocabulary and other words become obsolete. We call those words which were once common but are now used mainly to suggest an earlier period of time or style "archaic."

List words which are common now which might become archaic in 25 years.

Invent new words to describe things or events for which there are now no terms in our vocabulary.

Shuttle Service

It is 200 years from now and a new shuttle service to Mars is about to begin operation.

List all the ways you can think of to advertise the shuttle.

Design a poster advertising the service.

Time Capsule

List 20 items you would include in a time capsule to let future generations know what life was like for preteens and teens of the Twentieth Century.

1.
2.
3.
4.
5.
6.
7.
8.
9.
10.
11.
12.
13.
14.
15.
16.
17.
18.
19.
20.

Hypothesize

To hypothesize is to create an explanation that accounts for a set of facts. A hypothesis is really a guess that can be tested later by further investigation. For each of these situations, hypothesize and think of many possible reasons for the occurrence.

Situation #1: You go to the public library and on the door is a sign that says the library will be closed until further notice. You go to several neighboring towns and find the same situation in each. Why are the libraries closed?

_____

_____

_____

_____

_____

_____

Situation #2: The record that is number 1 on the Hit Parade will suddenly drop to number 50! What will cause the sudden decline in popularity?

_____

_____

_____

_____

_____

Ask a Seer

If you met someone who could foresee the future, what questions would you ask...

About World Affairs?

About Personal Matters?

Are there any things you definitely would *not* want to know?

Design a poster to advertise an "Ask a Seer" service.

Modern Flicks

In what ways would you like motion pictures of the Twenty-first Century to differ from those of the Twentieth Century?

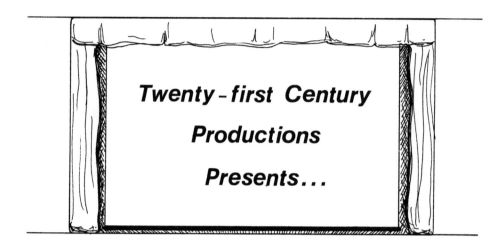

Name 2 movies which you recently viewed. List alternative titles for them.

Movie #1:_____   **Movie #2:**_____

1.   **1.**

2.   **2.**

3.   **3.**

4.   **4.**

Planning Helps

In order to reach our goals in the future (whether a minute later or a year later) we must plan ahead. For example, this realtor should have considered the needs of the clients before showing them a house! What kinds of things must each of these people consider in his or her daily planning?

A lawyer

An insurance salesperson

A teacher

A hair stylist

Analogies

Think about how the first two items in each are related. Then complete the analogies in interesting ways.

Today is to tomorrow as _____ is to _____.

Typewriter is to computer as _____ is to _____.

I am to my mother as _____ is to _____.

Wheels are to a car as _____ is to _____.

Read is to book as _____ is to _____.

Biplane is to rocket as _____ is to _____.

Then is to now as _____ is to _____.

Handwritten is to printed as _____ is to _____.

Yesterday is to today as _____ is to _____.

Intuition is to knowledge as _____ is to _____.

New Frontiers

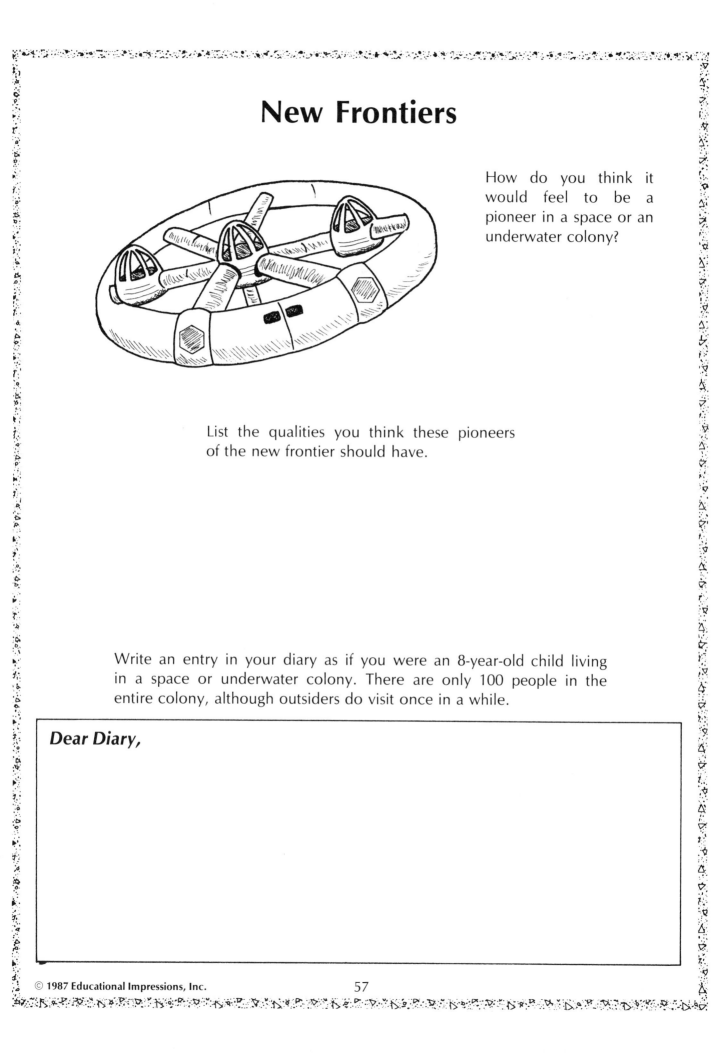

How do you think it would feel to be a pioneer in a space or an underwater colony?

List the qualities you think these pioneers of the new frontier should have.

Write an entry in your diary as if you were an 8-year-old child living in a space or underwater colony. There are only 100 people in the entire colony, although outsiders do visit once in a while.

Dear Diary,

Evolution

It is far into the future. Human beings have basically remained the same; however, they have developed a third eye!

Where is the third eye located?

What are the disadvantages of the third eye?

What are the advantages of the third eye?

Design eyeglasses for your 3-eyed human.

Resolutions

Every year many people list New Year's resolutions. They list all the things they have promised themselves to do—or in many cases *not* to do—during the coming year.

Make a list of resolutions you would like to make for the coming year. Do you think you will have the will power, initiative and perseverance to carry them out?

Resolution	Will Definitely Carry Out	Will Probably Carry Out	Will Probably Not Carry Out
1.			
2.			
3.			
4.			
5.			

I Need a Change

You want a change. Your parents will not buy you new furniture, so you decide to rearrange everything in your room. Think about your room the way it is now. Draw two **new** arrangements using the same furniture and accessories.

Arrangement #1

Arrangement #2

An Acrostic

An acrostic is a poem in which the first letter of each line spells a word or message. Write an acrostic about the future.

The Future

F _____

U _____

T _____

U _____

R _____

E _____

It doesn't have to rhyme!

What If...?

For each, hypothesize as to the possible consequences, advantages and disadvantages.

What if people could fly?

What if dogs could talk?

What if no one believed anything you said?

What if your clothes changed color with your mood?

Follow-up Activities

1. Design a postage stamp of the future to commemorate an important future event or accomplishment. Write a paragraph explaining what is being commemorated.

2. "Future Shock" is the condition of distress and disorientation brought on by an inability to cope with rapid societal and technological change. (From the book *Future Shock* by Alvin Toffler.) Suppose a human from the year 1887 found him/herself in the year 1987. Describe his/her feelings in terms of future shock.

3. Describe the 1980's from the perspective of a historian of the Twenty-second Century.

4. Think about what might happen if the nations of the world decided to have a universal language. Predict the consequences — both good and bad.

5. Analyze the possible benefits to be gained by future space exploration.

6. If you had the power to add an amendment to your federal constitution, what would it be? Explain why.

7. A utopia is an ideally perfect place. Describe a utopia as you envision it.

8. Research current trends and guess which occupations will be in high demand 10 years from now. Write a help-wanted ad for one of those positions. Include necessary qualifications, hours, salary and other pertinent information.

9. Think of ways to help solve one or more of the following problems: World Hunger, Energy Shortage, Illegal Drugs and the National Debt.

10. Think of some ways to improve the postal system.

11. Design a logo and a business card for your future career.

12. You decide to run for public office. Write a speech entitled, "If I'm Elected _____."

13. List the books written within the last ten years which you think will become classics.

14. Think of a new energy source.